THE PERSON
AND THE
COMMON GOOD

THE PERSON
AND THE
COMMON GOOD

BY
JACQUES MARITAIN

Translated by
JOHN J. FITZGERALD

UNIVERSITY OF NOTRE DAME PRESS

University of Notre Dame **Press**
Notre Dame, Indiana 46556
undpress.nd.edu
All Rights Reserved

First paperback edition © 1966 by University of Notre Dame
Published in the United States of America

Reprinted in 1972, 1977, 1985, 1991, 1995,
1999, 2002, 2006, 2009, 2012, 2015

∞ *This book is printed on acid-free paper.*

Acknowledgments

We have undertaken in this paper a reconsideration and development of two lectures: the first one, entitled "The Human Person and Society," was the Deneke Lecture, given at Oxford, May 9, 1939, and published in a limited edition (Paris, Desclée de Brouwer, 1940); the second one, entitled "The Person and the Individual," was given in Rome at the Pontifical Academy of Saint Thomas, November 22, 1945, and will appear in Volume XII of the Acts of this Academy. [Editor's Note: Chapters I–IV have appeared in "The Review of Politics" for October, 1946. Chapter V has not previously appeared in print.] We have also made such use of several of our earlier inquiries into this subject (Cf. *Freedom in the Modern World* and *The Rights of Man and Natural Law*) as to be able to present here a brief and, we trust, sufficiently clear synthesis of our position on a problem about which there have been numerous and (as I like to believe) involuntary misunderstandings.

Rome, Feb. 6, 1946.

J. M.

Contents

THE PERSON
AND THE
COMMON GOOD

I

Introductory

A MONG the truths of which contemporary thought stands in particular need and from which it could draw substantial profit is the doctrine of the distinction between individuality and personality. The essential importance of this distinction is revealed in the principles of St. Thomas. Unfortunately a right understanding of it is difficult to achieve and requires an exercise of metaphysical insight to which the contemporary mind is hardly accustomed.

Does society exist for each one of us, or does each one of us exist for society? Does the parish exist for the parishioner or the parishioner for the parish? This question, we feel immediately, involves two aspects, in each of which there must be some element of truth. A unilateral answer would only plunge us into error. Hence, we must disengage the formal principles of a truly comprehensive answer and describe the precise hierarchies of value which it implies. The Nineteenth Century experienced the errors of individualism. We have witnessed the development of a totalitarian or exclusively communal conception of society which took place by way of reaction. It was natural, then, that in a simultaneous reaction against both totaliarian and individualistic errors the concept of the human person, incorporated as such into society, be opposed to both the idea of the totalitarian state and that of the sovereignty of the individual. In consequence, minds related to widely differing schools of philosophic thought and quite uneven in intellectual exactitude and precision have sensed in the notion and term of "person" the solution sought. Whence, the "personalist" current which has developed in our time. Yet nothing can be more remote from the facts than the belief that "personalism" is one school or one doctrine. It is rather a phenomenon of reaction against two opposite errors, which inevitably contains elements of very unequal merits. Not a personalist doctrine, but personalist aspirations confront us. There are, at least, a dozen personalist doctrines, which, at times, have nothing more in common than the term "person." Some of them incline variously to one or the other of the contrary errors between which they take their stand. Some contemporary personalisms are Nietzschean in slant, others Proudhonian; some tend toward dictatorship, while others incline toward anarchy. A principal concern of Thomistic personalism is to avoid both excesses.

Our desire is to make clear the personalism rooted in the doctrine of St. Thomas and to separate, at the very outset, a social philosophy centered in the dignity of the human person from every social philosophy centered in the primacy of the individual and the private good. Thomistic personalism stresses the metaphysical distinction between individuality and personality.

Schwalm [1] and Garrigou-Lagrange [2] not only called attention to this distinction but were, to my knowledge, the first to show its fecundity in relation to contemporary moral and social problems. Following them, other Thomists—including

[1] R. P. Schwalm, O.P., *Leçons de Philosophie Sociale*, reedited in part under the title, *La Societé et l'Etat* (Paris, Flammarion, 1937).

[2] R. P. Garrigou-Lagrange, O.P., *La Philosophie de l'Etre et le Sens Commun* (1st edition, Paris, Beauchesne, 1904; 4th edition, Desclée de Brouwer, 1936).

Eberhard Welty [3] and myself [4]—have tried to make explicit its meaning and develop its consequences in social and political philosophy.

The true sense of the distinction has not always been grasped: first, as indicated above, because it is a difficult distinction (especially, perhaps, for sociologists, who are not always sensitive to the lures of the third degree of abstraction and wonder for what purpose they should first equip themselves as metaphysicians); and second, because certain minds, despite their metaphysical inclination, prefer confusion to distinction. This holds especially true when they are engaged in polemics and find it expedient to fabricate monsters which for the lack of anything better, in particular for the lack of references, are indiscriminately attributed to a host of anonymous adversaries.

[3] Eberhard Welty, O.P., *Gemeinschaft und Einzelmensch* (Pustet, Salzburg-Leipzig, 1935).

[4] Cf. *Three Reformers*, 1932; *True Humanism*, 1938; *Scholasticism and Politics*, 1940; *The Rights of Man and Natural Law*, 1943.

II

———————◆———————

The Positions of St. Thomas on the Ordination of the Person to Its Ultimate End

THE human person is ordained directly to God as to its absolute ultimate end. Its direct ordination to God transcends every created common good—both the common good of the political society and the intrinsic common good of the universe. Here is the fundamental truth governing the entire discussion—the truth in which nothing less than the very message of Christian wisdom in its triumph over Hellenic thought and every other pagan wisdom, henceforth toppled from their dominion, is involved. Here, too, St. Thomas Aquinas, following the precedent set by Albert the Great [5], did not take over the doctrine of Aristotle without correcting and transfiguring it.

"The most essential and the dearest aim of

[5] Cf. M. Rohner, O.P., "Kommentar des hl. Albertus Magnus zur Einführung in die Politik des Aristoteles," *Divus Thomas* (Friburg [Switzerland], 1932), pp. 95 ff.

15

Thomism is to make sure that the personal contact of all intellectual creatures with God, as well as their personal subordination to God, be in no way interrupted. Everything else—the whole universe and every social institution—must ultimately minister to this purpose; everything must foster and strengthen and protect the conversation of the soul, every soul, with God. It is characteristically Greek and pagan to interpose the universe between God and intellectual creatures." [6] It is to this essential concern for asserting and safeguarding the ordination, direct and personal, of each human soul to God that the principal points of doctrine, lying at the very heart of Thomism, are attached.

In the first place, there can be no question about the importance which St. Thomas unceasingly attributes to the consideration of the intrinsic order and "common good" of the cosmos—

[6] I. Th. Eschmann, O.P., "In Defense of Jacques Maritain," *The Modern Schoolman*, St. Louis University, May, 1945, p. 192. I am grateful to the author of these lines for having taken my defense in a debate in which I prefer to limit myself to a purely objective exposition; yet, in which, strangely enough, it has happened that, while criticizing ideas which are not mine, one has nevertheless, even when carefully refraining from uttering my name, allowed the reader to believe that I was indirectly referred to. I would like to hope that the present paper, while correcting some excessive expressions which I myself did not use, would put an end to the misunderstandings and confusions due to the original vice of such a controversy.

principally to establish the existence of Divine Providence against Greco-Arabian necessitarianism. Nonetheless, in comparing the intellectual substance and the universe, he emphasizes that intellectual creatures, though they, like all creatures, are ordained to the perfection of the created whole, are willed and governed for their own sakes. Divine Providence takes care of each one of them for its own sake and not at all as a mere cog in the machinery of the world. Obviously, this does not prevent them from being related first to God and then to the order and perfection of the created universe, of which they are the most noble constitutive parts.[7]

"They alone in the universe are willed for their own sake."[8] In other words, before they are related to the immanent common good of the uni-

---

[7] Each intellectual substance is made, first, for God, the separated common good of the universe, second, for the perfection of the order of the universe (not only as the universe of bodies but also as the universe of spirits), and third, for itself, that is, for the action (immanent and spiritual) by which it perfects itself and accomplishes its destiny. (Cf. *Sum. Theol.*, I, 65, 2, and Cajetan's commentary.) Using a distinction established further on, we may say that as individual or part, the intellectual substance is first willed and loved for the order of the universe and the perfection of the created whole; as person, it is first willed and loved for itself. Yet, like every creature, it differs from God, or Personality in pure act, more than it resembles Him. Hence, absolutely speaking, it is part or "individual" more than "person" and before it is a "person." (It is this that Kant failed to see.) It follows therefrom that, absolutely speaking, the intellectual sub-

verse, they are related to an infinitely greater good—the separated common Good, the divine transcendent Whole.[9] In intellectual creatures alone, Aquinas teaches further, is found the image of God. In no other creature, not even in the

stance is loved and willed for the order of the universe of creation before being loved and willed for itself. This in no wise hinders it, in contrast to irrational beings, from being really for itself and referred directly to God.

Let us add that if we pass to the supernatural order, the order of formal participation in the deity, this priority of the universe of created nature over the person is reversed. Each person is here willed and loved for its own sake, that is, to find bliss in God (He truly died for each of them), before being willed and loved for the order and perfection of *this* world or of the universe of nature and creation. "As He chose us in Him before the foundation of the world." *Ephes.* I, 4. (Whereas, "there is no election, nor a book of life as regards the life of nature." *Sum. Theol.* I, 24, 2 ad 2.) In the words of St. Augustine, the justification of the ungodly is a greater work than the creation of heaven and earth. In his teaching that the justification of the of the ungodly is "the greatest work of God," St. Thomas proposes the following objection: "The justification of the ungodly is ordained to the particular good of one man. But *the good of the universe is greater than the good of one man*, as is plain from Ethics I. Hence the creation of heaven and earth is a greater work than the justification of the ungodly." To it, he answers, "*The good of the universe is greater than the particular good of one, if we consider both in the same genus. But the good of grace in one is greater than the good of nature in the whole universe*," including the angelic natures. *Sum. Theol.* I-II, 113, 9, ad 2.

On the other hand, in this same supernatural order, each person, willed and loved for itself and for the communication of the divine goodness which is made to it, is also and *first of all*, willed and loved (by the same act of transcendent love which grasps all at once the whole and the part) for the communication of the divine goodness which is made to the whole city of the blessed in the sense that each of its members beholds the uncreated essence according to the multiple degrees of their participation in the light of glory.

18

universe as a whole, is this found. To be sure, with regard to the extension and variety according to which the divine attributes are manifested, there is more participated similitude of the divine perfections in the whole totality of creatures.

Finally if in the order of grace, the person itself desires God as its good, it does so in loving God for Himself, more than itself, and in willing the good of God more than its own proper good. Indeed, if it wills God for *itself,* it is not for the sake of itself as final reason but rather for the sake of God purely and simply as final reason. (Cf. the invaluable commentary of Cajetan on the relations between Hope and Charity, II-II, 17, 5.

[8] Cf. *Sum. Contra Gentiles,* III, 112: "Intellectual creatures are ruled by God as though He cared for them for their own sake, while other creatures are ruled as being directed to rational creatures. . . . Therefore the intellectual nature alone is requisite for its own sake in the universe, and all others for its sake." *Ibid.,* III, 113: "The rational soul is capable of perpetuity, not only in respect of the species, like other creatures, but also in respect of the individual . . . Rational creatures alone are directed by God to their actions for the sake, not only of the species, but also of the individual. . . . Rational creatures alone are directed by God providence as being for its own sake governed and cared for, and not, as other corruptible creatures, for the sake of the species only. For the individual that is governed only for the sake of the species is not governed for its own sake, whereas the rational creature is governed for its own sake . . . Accordingly, rational creatures alone are directed by God to their actions for the sake, not only of the species, but also of the individual."

[9] That the extrinsic or separated common good of a multitude, to which it is ordained, is greater than the immanent common good of the multitude is a universal principle: . . . "Just as the good of a multitude is greater than the good of a unit in that multitude, so it is less than the extrinsic good to which that multitude is directed, as the good order of an army is less than the (objective) good (the defeat of the enemy) of its commander-in-chief. In like manner the good of ecclesiastical unity, to which schism is opposed, is less than the good of Divine truth, to which unbelief is opposed." *Sum. Theol.* II-II, 39, 2, ad 2.

19

But considering the degree of perfection with which each one approaches God according to its capacity, the intellectual creature, which is capable of the supreme good, is more like unto the divine perfection than the whole universe in its entirety. For it alone is properly the image of God.[10]

Elsewhere, the Angelic Doctor writes that the good of grace of one person is worth more than the good of the whole universe of nature. For, precisely because it alone is capable of the supreme good, because it alone is the image of God, the intellectual creature alone is capable of grace. He also teaches that the natural knowledge of the angels does not extend to the secrets of the heart, even though it encompasses *de jure* all the things of this world. The reason is, as John of St. Thomas explained, because the free act of the human person, considered in its pure and secret intimacy as a free act, is not of this world. By its liberty, the human person transcends the stars and all the world of nature.

In the second place concerning the possession itself of the ultimate end, St. Thomas teaches that in the beatific vision each blessed soul, knowing

[10] *Sum. Theol.*, I, 93, 2.

God as He is and as it itself is known by Him,[11] grasps the Divine Essence and becomes God intentionally in the most immediate act conceivable. In this act, the Divine Essence itself assumes the role of "impressed species" in the human intellect. The "light of glory" enables the intellect to know in a direct intuition, without any created intermediary, without even the mediation of an idea, the very Being whose intelligibility in pure act is *per se* proportionate only to the Intellect in pure act. The divine beatitude enjoys eternally the exhaustive knowledge of those uncreated depths. The beatific vision is therefore the supremely personal act by which the soul, transcending absolutely every sort of created common good, enters into the very bliss of God and draws its life from the uncreated Good, the divine essence itself, the uncreated common Good of the three Divine Persons.

Were there but a single soul to enjoy God thus, it would still be blessed, even though it would not have to share this beatitude with any other creature.[12] Ordained to Him who is the Good by His essence and the Good by essence, it has, as

[11] Saint Paul, *I Cor.*, 13:12: "Now I know in part; but then I shall know even as I am known."
[12] *Sum. Theol.*, I-II, 4, 8, ad 3.

the object of its vision and the substance of its beatitude, God as He is in Himself. Together, God and the soul, are two in one; two natures in a single vision and a single love. The soul is filled with God. It is in society with God. With Him, it possesses a common good, the divine Good Itself. And thus the adage "Goods are common among friends" holds for it. "Absolutely speaking that love, since it is like friendship, is perfect love by which God loves His creatures not only as the artisan loves his work but also with a certain friendly association, as friend loves friend, in as much as He draws them into the community of His own enjoyment in order that their glory and beatitude may reside in that very thing by which He Himself is blessed." [13] The beatific vision, good so personal, knowledge so incommunicable that the soul of the blessed cannot even express it to itself in an interior word, is the most perfect, the most secret and the most divine solitude with God.

Yet, it is the most open, most generous and

[13] "*Deus non tantum diligit creaturam sicut artifex opus, sed etiam quadam amicabili societate, sicut amicus amicum, inquantum trahit eos in societatem suae fruitionis, ut in hoc eorum sit gloria et beatitudo, quo Deus beatus est.*" Saint Thomas, 2 *Sent.*, d. 26, 1. ad 2.

most inhabited solitude. Because of it, another society is formed—the society of the multitude of blessed souls, each of which on its own account beholds the divine essence and enjoys the same uncreated Good. They love mutually in God. The uncreated common Good, in which they all participate, constitutes the common good of the celestial city in which they are congregated. It is this society of which St. Augustine writes: "The peace of the celestial city is the perfectly ordered and harmonious enjoyment of God, and of one another in God." [14] According to St. Thomas, it is neither essential to nor necessarily required by perfect beatitude; this society accompanies it: "Friendship stands a concomitant, as it were, of perfect beatitude." [15]

Let us note further that, though God is the "separated common good" of the universe, the intellectual creature is related, primarily as to the object of its beatitude, not to God as the common good of the universe of nature and creation, but to God in the transcendence of his own mystery; to God as Deity, conceptually ineffable, expressible only in the Uncreated Word; to God

[14] *De Civ. Dei*, XIX, 13.
[15] *Sum. Theol.*, I-II, 4, 8 ad 3.

as common good of the divine Persons and of the souls which have entered by participation into the universe of the Deity. It is only consequentially, because God is the common good of the multitude of beatified creatures which all communicate with Him, that they communicate in His love with one another, *outside of the vision,* by all the created communications of mutual knowledge and mutual charity and common adoration, which flow from the vision; by those exchanges and that celestial conversation, those illuminations and that common praise of God, which render back unto each of them the goods which they have in common. The eminently personal act in which each beholds the divine essence at once transcends their blessed community and provides it with a foundation.

A third point of doctrine, concerning the superiority of the speculative over the practical intellect, likewise constitutes an essential thesis of Thomism and confirms what we have just observed. For St. Thomas, beatitude, which consists formally in the vision, pertains to the speculative and not to the practical intellect. The object of the practical intellect is a practical good, a good to be done, a good which, however lofty it may be, remains inferior to the truth to be known and the subsistent Good itself. In consequence, the resemblance to God is less in the practical than in the speculative intellect. "The asserted likeness of the practical intellect to God is one of proportion; that is to say, by reason of its standing in relation to what it knows (and brings into existence) as God does to what He knows (creatively). But the likeness of the speculative to God is one of union and information; which is a much greater likeness." [16] Now this much more perfect similitude with God, characteristic of the speculative intellect, is accomplished by a personal and solitary act of each one's intellect.

The good and the end of the speculative intellect are of themselves superior to the good and the end of the practical intellect. Hence, they are superior to every created common good, however eminent it may be. For the highest object of the practical intellect is a common good to be realized. [17] "By the practical intellect," writes St. Thomas, "one directs oneself and others towards the end as it is exemplified in him who directs the multitude. But by the fact that a man contem-

[16] *Sum. Theol.*, I-II, 3, 5, ad 1.
[17] *Sum. Theol.*, II-II, 47, 2 ad 11.

plates, he directs himself alone towards the end of contemplation. The end itself of the speculative intellect surpasses as much the good of the practical intellect as the personal attainment of this speculative end, transcends the common accomplishment of the good of the practical intellect. For this reason, the most perfect beatitude resides in the speculative intellect." [18] These two texts, which we have just quoted and which yield, as has been noted, one of the keys to the "personalism" of a doctrine that also asserts, at each degree of the analogy of being, the primacy of the common good, introduce us to the second great Thomistic theme which we wish to recall in the first part of this study, namely, the preeminence of the contemplative over the political life.

This doctrine is so well known that a brief recollection will suffice here. Because of its perfect immanence and its high degree of immateriality, contemplative activity is the highest of human activities. It binds man to things divine. It is better than life on the human scale. In supernatural contemplation it takes place according to a mode which is itself superhuman, through

[18] 3 *Sent.*, 35, I, 4 sol. 1c et ad 2 et 3, 4 *Sent.*, 49, I, 1, sol. 3 ad 1.

the connaturality of love with God and the action of the gifts of the Holy Spirit. It makes of the transfigured soul one spirit with God. It is supreme and active repose, activity essentially theological—received in its entirety from God, an imperfect and crucified beginning of beatitude. To it are ordained the moral virtues, which are at the service of wisdom as the valet is at the service of the king. It is from it, when the soul is perfect, that the works of the active life must overflow, at least as to the mode of their accomplishment. And if a man be called to abandon his contemplation to come to the aid of his brothers or to serve the good of the community, the reason for this call is not at all because the good of the practical order is of itself superior to his solitary contemplation. He must accept it only because the order of charity can require that an urgent necessity of a less elevated good, in the circumstances, be given priority. In truth, such a man if he has entered upon the pathways of the perfect life, would be abandoning rather the conditions and leisure of contemplation than contemplation itself, which would remain, in the recesses of the soul, the source from which his practical activity would descend into human affairs.

27

Such is St. Thomas' doctrine on this crucial problem of action and contemplation—a problem at the very heart of social philosophy, a problem the solution of which is of prime importance to every civilization worthy of the name. With an incomparable incisiveness, it affirms the human person's vocation to contemplation. It is a doctrine of the primacy of the act, of the act *par excellence*, the act of the spirit; it is, for that very reason, a doctrine of the primacy of that which is spiritual and most eminently personal: "Just as that which is already perfect is superior to that which is practiced for perfection, so the life of the solitaries," of those who, in the words of Aristotle, are not as beasts but as gods, "is superior to life in society." [19] The contemplative life is better than the political life.

This doctrine is at the same time a doctrine of the primacy of the common good. No one more than St. Thomas has emphasized the primacy of the common good in the practical or political order of the life of the city, as in every order, where, in relation to a same category of good, [20]

---

[19] *Sum. Theol.*, II-II, 188, 8.
[20] "The good of the universe is greater than the particular good of one, if we consider both in the same genus." *Sum. Theol.*, I-II, 113, 9, ad 2.

the distinction between the private and common good is found. At every opportunity, he repeats the maxim of Aristotle that the good of the whole is "more divine" than the good of the parts. Unceasingly he strives to preserve this *dictum authenticum,* applied according to the most diverse degrees of analogy. *A fortiori,* then, does he give it its full value in strictly social matters. Because the common good is the *human* common good,[21] it includes within its essence, as we shall see later, the service of the human person.[22] The adage of the superiority of the common good is

[21] "The end of politics is the human good; it is the highest end in human things." St. Thomas, in *Eth.* I, 2.

[22] As expressed by Pope Pius XII in His Christmas Message of 1942, "The origin and the primary scope of social life is the conservation, development and perfection of the human person, helping him to realize accurately the demands and values of religion and culture set by the creator for every man and for all mankind, both as a whole and in its natural ramifications." (Translation published by *The Catholic Mind,* Jan. 1943.)

From the Encyclical *Mystici Corporis:* "In a natural body the principle of unity so unites the parts that each lacks its own individual subsistence; on the contrary in the Mystical Body that mutual union, though intrinsic, links the members by a bond which leaves to each intact his own personality. Besides, if we examine the relation existing between the several members and the head, in every physical, living body, all the different members are ultimately destined to the good of the whole alone; while every moral association of men, if we look to its ultimate usefulness, is in the end directed to the advancement of all and of every single member. For they are persons, *utpote personae sunt.*" (Prepared by Joseph J. Bluett, S.J., The America Press, New York.) This passage is truly the charter of the Christian doctrine on the person.

understood in its true sense only in the measure that the common good itself implies a reference to the human person. As La Pira [23] rightly observed, the worst errors concerning society are born of the confusion between the substantial whole of the biological organism and the collective whole, itself composed of persons, of society. But to understand these things more profoundly, we must uncover the metaphysical roots of the question and engage in more subtle considerations about the individual and the person.

[23] Giorgio La Pira, "Problemi della persona umana," *Acta Pont. Academiae Romanae Sancti Thomas Aq.*, vol. VIII (Rome—Torino, Marietti, 1945).

III

Individuality and Personality

IS NOT the *person* the self? Is not *my person my self?* Let us consider the singular contradictions to which this term and notion of *self* give rise.

Pascal asserts that "the self is detestable." This expression is a common-place of Pascalian literature. In every-day language when we represent someone as "self-assertive," do we not mean that he is self-centered, imperious and dominating— scarcely capable of friendship? A distinguished contemporary artist once remarked, "I do not like *others*"; a remark that reveals a strongly asserted personality. In this sense, we might construe personality to consist in self-realization achieved at the expense of others. So construed, personality would always imply a certain selfishness or imperviousness because no place remains for anything or anyone else in the man who is busy with himself.

On the other hand, is it not a serious reproach to assert of a man that he has no personality? Do not heroes and saints impress us as men who have reached the heights of personality as well as generosity? Nothing great is accomplished in the world save through a heroic fidelity to some truth which a man who says "I" sees and proclaims; a heroic fidelity to some mission which he, himself, a human person, must fulfill; of which, perhaps, he alone is aware and for which he lays down his life.

But let us turn to the Gospel; no personality is more magnificently asserted than that of Christ. Revealed dogma tells us that it is the personality itself of the Uncreated Word.

Here, in contrast to the expression of Pascal that "the self is detestable," the words of St. Thomas come to mind; "the person is that which is most noble and most perfect in all of nature." [24] Whereas Pascal teaches that "the self is detestable," St. Thomas teaches that whosoever loves God must love himself for the sake of God, must

[24] "Person signifies what is most perfect in all nature—that is, a subsistent individual of a rational nature." *Sum. Theol.*, I, 29, 3.

love his own soul and body with a love of charity. Concern for self—or what contemporary psychology calls introversion—can wreak much havoc. Those who have been reared in a strict Puritanism are said to complain of a suffering, a kind of interior paralysis, created by *self-consciousness*. On the other hand, philosophers, above all St. Augustine and in modern times Hegel, teach that self-knowledge is a privilege of the spirit; that much human progress consists in the progress of consciousness of self.

What do these contradictions mean? They mean that the human being is caught between two poles; a material pole, which, in reality, does not concern the true person but rather the shadow of personality or what, in the strict sense, is called *individuality*, and a spiritual pole, which does concern *true personality*.

It is to the material pole, the individual become the center of all, that the expression of Pascal refers. St. Thomas' expression on the contrary refers to the spiritual pole, the person, source of liberty and bountifulness. Thus, we are confronted with the distinction between *individuality* and *personality*.

This is no new distinction but a classical distinction belonging to the intellectual heritage of mankind. In Hindu philosophy, it corresponds to the distinction between the *ego* and the *self*. It is fundamental in the doctrine of St. Thomas. Contemporary sociological and spiritual problems have made it particularly timely. Widely different schools of thought appeal to it; the Thomists, certain disciples of Proudhon, Nicolas Berdiaeff and those philosophers who, prior to the invasion of the young existentialist group, already spoke of "existential philosophy." Hence it is all important to distinguish between the individual and the person. It is no less important to understand the distinction correctly.

. . . .

Let us consider individuality first. Outside of the mind, only individual realities exist.[25] Only they are capable of exercising the act of existing. Individuality is opposed to the state of universality which things have in the mind. It designates that concrete state of unity and indivision, required by existence, in virtue of which every actually or possibly existing nature can posit itself in existence as distinct from other beings.

[25] And also collective realities constituted of individuals, such as society (*unum per accidens*).

34

The angels are individual essences; the Divine Essence, in Its sovereign unity and simplicity, is supremely individual. Pure forms or pure spirits are, of themselves or by reason of that which constitutes their substantial intelligibility, in the state of individuality. For this reason, St. Thomas says that each angel differs from any other as the whole species of lions differs from the whole species of horses or from the whole species of eagles. In other words, each angel differs specifically from every other; each is an individual by the very form (absolutely free from any matter) in which its being consists and which constitutes it in its species.

The situation of terrestrial things, material beings, is quite different. According to the Angelic Doctor, their individuality is rooted in matter in as much as matter requires the occupation in space of a position distinct from every other position. Matter itself is a kind of non-being, a mere potency or ability to receive forms and undergo substantial mutations; in short, an avidity for being. In every being made of matter, this pure potency bears the impress of a metaphysical energy—the "form" or "soul"—which constitutes with it a substantial unit and determines

35

this unit to be that which it is. By the fact that it is ordained to inform matter, the form finds itself particularized in such and such a being which shares the same specific nature with other beings equally immersed in spatiality.

According to this doctrine, the human soul, together with the matter which it informs, constitutes one substance, which is both carnal and spiritual. The soul is not, as Descartes believed, a thing—thought—existing on its own as a complete being, and the body another thing—extension—existing on its own as a complete being. Soul and matter are the two substantial co-principles of the same being, of one and the same reality, called man. Because each soul is intended to animate a particular body, which receives its matter from the germinal cells, with all their hereditary content, from which it develops, and because, further, each soul has or *is* a substantial relation to a particular body, it has within its very substance the individual characteristics which differentiate it from every other human soul.

In man, as in all other corporeal beings, the atom, the molecule, the plant, the animal, individuality has its first ontological roots in matter. Such is St. Thomas' doctrine on the individuality

of material things. This common characteristic of
all existents, namely, that in order to exist they
must be undivided and distinct from every other
existent, does not in corporeal beings, as in pure
spirits, derive from the form which constitutes
them at such and such a degree of specific intelligibility. In them, this common characteristic is
realized below the level of intelligibility in act
which is proper to the separated form—whether
it is separated in real existence or by the abstrac-
tive operation of the mind. Corporeal beings are
individual because of "matter with its quantity
designated." Their specific form and their essence are not individual by reason of their own
entity but by reason of their transcendental relation to matter understood as implying position in
space.

We have characterized matter as an avidity for
being, having of itself no determination and de-
riving all of its determinations from form. In each
of us, individuality, being that which excludes
from oneself all that other men are, could be
described as the narrowness of the ego, forever
threatened and forever eager *to grasp for itself*.
Such narrowness in flesh animated by a spirit
derives from matter. As a material individuality,

man has only a precarious unity, which tends to
be scattered in a multiplicity. For of itself, matter
is inclined to disintegration just as space is inclined to division. As an individual, each of us is
a fragment of a species, a part of the universe, a
unique point in the immense web of cosmic, eth-
nical, historical forces and influences—and bound
by their laws. Each of us is subject to the deter-
minism of the physical world. Nonetheless, each
of us is also a person and, as such, is not con-
trolled by the stars. Our whole being subsists in
virtue of the subsistence of the spiritual soul
which is in us a principle of creative unity, independence and liberty.

.   .   .   .

We have sketched briefly the theory of individuality. Personality is a much deeper mystery,
and to probe the depths of its meaning is consid-
erably more difficult. Perhaps the most apposite
approach to the philosophical discovery of personality is the study of the relation between
personality and love.

"Not the person but only its qualities do we
love," Pascal has said. This is a false statement,
and exhibits in Pascal a trace of the very ration-
alism against which he strove to protect himself.

Love is not concerned with qualities. They are not the object of our love. We love the deepest, most substantial and hidden, the most *existing* reality of the beloved being. This is a metaphysical center deeper than all the qualities and essences which we can find and enumerate in the beloved. The expressions of lovers are unending because their object is ineffable.

Love seeks out this center, not, to be sure, as separated from its qualities, but as one with them. This is a center inexhaustible, so to speak, of existence, bounty and action; capable of giving and of *giving itself*; capable of receiving not only this or that gift bestowed by another, but even another self as a gift, another self which bestows itself. This brief consideration of love's own law brings us to the metaphysical problem of the person. For love is not concerned with qualities or natures or essences but with *persons*.

"Thou art *thyself*," says Juliet "though not a Montague . . . Romeo, doff thy name, and for thy name, which is not part of thee, take all myself."

To bestow oneself, one must first exist; not indeed, as a sound, which passes through the air, or an idea, which crosses the mind, but as a thing, which subsists and exercises existence for itself. Such a being must exist not only as other things do, but eminently, in self-possession, holding itself in hand, master of itself. In short, it must be endowed with a spiritual existence, capable of containing itself thanks to the operations of the intellect and freedom, capable of super-existing by way of knowledge and of love. For this reason, the metaphysical tradition of the West defines the person in terms of independence, as a reality which, subsisting spiritually, constitutes a universe unto itself, a relatively independent whole within the great whole of the universe, facing the transcendent whole which is God. For the same reason, this tradition finds in God the sovereign Personality whose existence itself consists in a pure and absolute super-existence by way of intellection and love. Unlike the concept of the individuality of corporeal things, the concept of personality is related not to matter but to the deepest and highest dimensions of being. Its roots are in the spirit inasmuch as the spirit holds itself in existence and superabounds in existence. Metaphysically considered, personality is, as the Thomistic School rightly asserts,[26] "subsistence,"

[26] Cf. My work *The Degrees of Knowledge*, Appendix IV.

the ultimate achievement by which the creative influx seals, within itself, a nature face to face with the whole order of existence so that the existence which it receives is *its own* existence and *its own* perfection. Personality is the subsistence of the spiritual soul communicated to the human composite. Because, in our substance, it is an imprint or seal which enables it to possess its existence, to perfect and give itself freely, personality testifies to the generosity or expansiveness in being which an incarnate spirit derives from its spiritual nature and which constitutes, within the secret depths of our ontological structure, a source of dynamic unity, of unification from within.

Personality, therefore, signifies interiority to self. And because it is the spirit in man which takes him, in contrast to the plant and animal, beyond the threshold of independence properly so called, and of interiority to oneself, the subjectivity of the person has nothing in common with the isolated unity, without doors or windows, of the Leibnizian monad. It requires the communications of knowledge and love. By the very fact that each of us is a person and expresses himself to himself, each of us requires com-

41

munication with *other* and *the others* in the order of knowledge and love. Personality, of its essence, requires a dialogue in which souls really communicate. Such communication is rarely possible. For this reason, personality in man seems to be bound to the experience of affliction even more profoundly than to the experience of creative effort. The person is directly related to the absolute. For only in the absolute is it able to enjoy its full sufficiency. Its spiritual homeland is the whole universe of the absolute and of those indefectible goods which are as the pathways to the absolute Whole which transcends the world.

Finally, we turn to religious thought for the last word and find that the deepest layer of the human person's dignity consists in its property of resembling God—not in a general way after the manner of all creatures, but in a *proper* way. It is the *image of God.* For God is spirit and the human person proceeds from Him in having as principle of life a spiritual soul capable of knowing, loving and of being uplifted by grace to participation in the very life of God so that, in the end, it might know and love Him as He knows and loves Himself.

.   .   .   .

If our description is adequate, such are the two metaphysical aspects of the human being, individuality and personality, together with their proper ontological features. However evident it may seem, in order to avoid misunderstandings and nonsense, we must emphasize that they are not two separate things. There is not in me one reality, called my individual, and another reality, called my person. One and the same reality is, in a certain sense an individual, and, in another sense, a person. Our whole being is an individual by reason of that in us which derives from matter, and a person by reason of that in us which derives from spirit. Similarly, the whole of a painting is a physico-chemical mixture by reason of the coloring stuff of which it is made, and the whole of it is a work of beauty by reason of the painter's art.

Of course, material individuality is not something evil in itself. Obviously as the very condition of our existence, it is something good. But it is precisely as related to personality that individuality is good. Evil arises when, in our action, we give preponderance to the individual aspect of our being. For although each of our acts is simultaneously the act of ourselves as an individual and as a person, yet, by the very fact that it is free and involves our whole being, each act is linked in a movement towards the supreme center to which personality tends, or in a movement towards that dispersion into which, if left to itself, material individuality is inclined to fall.

It should be noted here that man must realize through his will that of which his nature is but the sketch. In terms of a commonplace—and a very profound one—which goes back to Pindar, man must become what he is. And this he must do at a sorrowful cost and with formidable risks. He himself, in the moral order, must win his liberty and his personality. In other words, as observed above, his action can follow the bent either of personality or of material individuality.[27] If the development occurs in the direction of material individuality, it will be orientated towards the detestable ego whose law is *to grasp* or absorb for itself. At the same time personality, as such, will tend to be adulterated and to dissolve. But if the development occurs in the direction of spiritual personality, man will be orientated towards the generous self of the heroes and saints. Thus, man will be truly a person only in

[27] Cf. R. Garrigou-Lagrange, *Le Sens Commun, la Philosophie de l'Etre et les Formules Dogmatiques,* 3e et 4e éditions, 3e Partie, Chap. II.

so far as the life of the spirit and of liberty reigns over that of the senses and passions.

Here we are confronted with the crucial problem of the education of man. There are some who confound the person with the individual. To effectuate the development of personality and the freedom of expansion to which it aspires, they reject all asceticism; these would have the tree bear fruit without having been pruned. Instead of self-fulfilment, the man, thus educated, achieves only dispersion and disintegration. The heart becomes atrophied and the senses exacerbated, or else all that is most human in man recoils into a vacuum veiled in frivolity.

Others misunderstand the distinction between the individual and the person; they mistake it for a separation. These believe that there are two separate beings in each of us, the one—the individual, the other—the person. Their motto is: "Death to the individual, long live the person!" The pity is that, in killing the individual, they also kill the person. The *despotic* conception of the progress of the human being is no whit better than the *anarchistic* conception. Its ideal seems to be first, remove the heart—painlessly if possible —then replace it with the heart of an angel. The

45

second is by far the more difficult operation, and succeeds more rarely. Instead of the authentic person, exhibiting the mysterious visage of the Creator, a mask appears, the austere mask of the Pharisee.

It is the interior principle, namely, nature and grace, which matters most in the education and progress of the human being, just as it is an inner principle which matters most in organic growth. Our instruments are simply the aids; our art is but the servant and cooperator of this interior principle. The whole function of this art is to prune and to trim—operations in which both the individual and the person are interested—in such wise that, within the intimacy of the human being, the gravity of individuality diminishes and that of true personality and its generosity increases. Such an art, to be sure, is difficult.

IV

The Person and Society

IN OUR treatment of the characteristic features
of the person, we noted that personality tends
by nature to communion. This frequently mis-
understood point should be emphasized. For the
person requires membership in a society in virtue
both of its dignity and its needs. Animal groups
or colonies are called societies only in an improper sense. They are collective wholes constituted of mere individuals. Society in the proper
sense, human society, is a society of persons. A
city worthy of the name is a city of human
persons. The social unit is the person.

But why is it that the person, as person, seeks
to live in society? It does so, first, because of its
very perfections, as person, and its inner urge to
the communications of knowledge and love which
require relationship with other persons. In its

radical generosity, the human person tends to overflow into social communications in response to the law of superabundance inscribed in the depths of being, life, intelligence and love. It does so secondly because of its needs or deficiencies, which derive from its material individuality. In this respect, unless it is integrated in a body of social communications, it cannot attain the fullness of its life and accomplishment. Society appears, therefore, to provide the human person with just those conditions of existence and development which it needs. It is not by itself alone that it reaches its plenitude but by receiving essential goods from society.

Here the question is not only of his material needs, of bread, clothes and shelter, for which man requires the help of his fellowmen, but also, and above all, of the help which he ought to be given to do the work of reason and virtue, which responds to the specific feature of his being. To reach a certain degree of elevation in knowledge as well as a certain degree of perfection in moral life, man needs an education and the help of other men. In this sense, Aristotle's statement that man is by nature a political animal holds with great exactitude: man is a political animal because he is a rational animal, because reason requires development through character training, education and the cooperation of other men, and because society is thus indispensable to the accomplishment of human dignity.

.   .   .   .

There is a correlation between this notion of the *person* as social unit and the notion of the *common good* as the end of the social whole. They imply one another. The common good is common because it is received in persons, each one of whom is as a mirror of the whole. Among the bees, there is a public good, namely, the good functioning of the hive, but not a common good, that is, a good received and communicated.[28] The end of society, therefore, is neither the individual good nor the collection of the in-

[28] In an animal society, the *individual* is not a person; hence, has not the value of a moral "whole" and is not a subject of right. If the good of the whole profits the parts, as the good of the body profits its members, it does not in the sense that it is turned back or *redistributed* to them. It is merely in order that the whole itself might subsist and be better served that its parts are kept alive or maintained in good condition. Thus, they partake of the good of the whole but only *as parts* of the whole. Indeed, how could it be the good of the whole without thereby profiting the parts which compose the whole (except when it requires the sacrifice of this or that part which then spontaneously exposes itself to peril, as the hand to save the body, because by nature it loves the whole more than itself, cf. Cajetan, in I, 60, 5)? Such a good is a common good in a general and improperly social sense. It is not the *formally social* common good, with which we are con-

dividual goods of each of the persons who constitute it. Such a conception would dissolve society as such to the advantage of its parts, and would amount to either a frankly anarchistic conception, or the old disguised anarchistic conception of individualistic materialism in which the whole function of the city is to safeguard the liberty of each; thus giving to the strong full freedom to oppress the weak.

The end of society is the good of the community, of the social body. But if the good of the social body is not understood to be a common good of *human persons,* just as the social body itself is a whole of human persons, this conception also would lead to other errors of a totalitarian type. The common good of the city is neither the mere collection of private goods, nor

cerned in this paper. It is common to the whole and to the parts only in an improper sense, for it does not profit the parts *for themselves* at the same time as *for the whole* according to the characteristic exigencies of a whole constituted of persons. It is rather the proper good of the whole—not foreign to the parts, to be sure, but benefiting them only for its own sake and the sake of the whole.

This kind of common good of an animal society is analogically a "bonum honestum" (reached *materialiter et executive, sub directione Dei auctoris naturae*), but in its proper order, where the whole is composed of individuals who are not persons. The common good, formally social, of human society, in order to be truly common good and to attain, as common good, the character of "bonum honestum," implies redistribution to the persons as persons.

the proper good of a whole which, like the species with respect to its individuals or the hive with respect to its bees, relates the parts to itself alone and sacrifices them to itself. It is the good *human* life of the multitude, of a multitude of persons; it is their communion in good living. It is therefore common to both *the whole and the parts* into which it flows back and which, in turn, must benefit from it. Unless it would vitiate itself, it implies and requires recognition of the fundamental rights of persons and those of the domestic society in which the persons are more primitively engaged than in the political society. It includes within itself as principal value, the highest access, compatible with the good of the whole, of the persons to their life of person and liberty of expansion, as well as to the communications of generosity consequent upon such expansion. If, as we intend to emphasize later, the common good of the city implies an intrinsic ordination to something which transcends it, it is because it requires, by its very essence and within its proper sphere, communication or redistribution to the persons who constitute society. It presupposes the persons and flows back upon them, and, in this sense, is achieved in them.

Thus, that which constitutes the common good of political society is not only: the collection of public commodities and services—the roads, ports, schools, etc., which the organization of common life presupposes; a sound fiscal condition of the state and its military power; the body of just laws, good customs and wise institutions, which provide the nation with its structure; the heritage of its great historical remembrances, its symbols and its glories, its living traditions and cultural treasures. The common good includes all of these and something much more besides—something more profound, more concrete and more human. For it includes also, and above all, the whole sum itself of these; a sum which is quite different from a simple collection of juxtaposed units. (Even in the mathematical order, as Aristotle points out, 6 is not the same as $3 + 3$.) It includes the sum or sociological integration of all the civic conscience, political virtues and sense of right and liberty, of all the activity, material prosperity and spiritual riches, of unconsciously operative hereditary wisdom, of moral rectitude, justice, friendship, happiness, virtue and heroism in the individual lives of its members. For these things all are, in a certain measure, *communicable* and so revert to each member, helping him to perfect his life and liberty of person. They all constitute the good human life of the multitude.

Let us note in passing that the common good is not only a system of advantages and utilities but also a rectitude of life, an end, good in itself or, as the Ancients expressed it, a *bonum honestum*. For, on the one hand, to assure the existence of the multitude is something morally good in itself; on the other hand, the existence, thus assured, must be the just and morally good existence of the community. Only on condition that it is according to justice and moral goodness is the common good what it is, namely, the good of a people and a city, rather than of a mob of gangsters and murderers. For this reason, perfidy, the scorn of treaties and the sworn oath, political assassination and unjust war, even though they be *useful* to a government and procure some fleeting advantages for the peoples who make use of them, tend by their nature as political acts— acts involving in some degree the common action —to the destruction of the common good.

The common good is something ethically good. Included in it, as an essential element, is the maximum possible development, here and now, of the persons making up the united multitude to the end of forming a people, organized not by force alone but by justice. Historical conditions and the still inferior development of humanity make difficult the full achievement of the end of social life. But the end to which it tends is to procure the common good of the multitude in such a way that the concrete person gains the greatest possible measure, compatible with the good of the whole, of real independence from the servitudes of nature. The economic guarantees of labor and capital, political rights, the moral virtues and the culture of the mind, all contribute to the realization of this independence.

A twofold observation is pertinent here. On the one hand, the common good of civil society implies that the whole man is engaged in it. Unlike a farmers' cooperative or a scientific association, which require the commitment of only part of the interests of the members, civil society requires the citizens to commit their lives, properties and honor. On the other hand, it should be noted that the idea of the "perfect society," to which the idea of the common good of political society is linked, has experienced many adventures in the course of history; it may even be doubted whether it has ever been truly realized within the limits of any particular social group. Contemporary states are more remote from the ideal type of the "perfect society" than the city of Aristotle's day or the body politic in the time of Suarez. The common good in our day is certainly not just the common good of the nation and has not yet succeeded in becoming the common good of the civilized world community. It tends, however, unmistakably towards the latter. For this reason, it would seem appropriate to consider the common good of a state or nation as merely an area, among many similar areas, in which the common good of the whole civilized society achieves greater density.

We have emphasized the sociability of the person and the properly *human* nature of the common good. We have seen that it is a good according to the requirements of justice; that it must flow back upon persons, and that it includes, as its principal value, the access of persons to their liberty of expansion.

We have not yet considered what might be termed the typical paradox of social life. Here again we shall find the distinction of the individual and the person. For this paradox results from the fact, already noted, that each of us is in his entirety an individual and in his entirety a person.

At this point, a few metaphysical and also theological observations would help to assure the correct development of the discussion. Let us recall that the idea of person is an analogical idea which is realized fully and absolutely only in its supreme analogue, God, the Pure Act. Let us recall further that, for St. Thomas, the intelligible value of "whole," "totality," is indissolubly bound to that of person. It is a fundamental thesis of Thomism that the person as such is a whole. The concept of part is opposed to that of person." [29]

To say, then, that society is a whole composed

[29] In III *Sent.* d. 5, 3, 2. St. Thomas, in this text, refers to the human composite (*unum per se*) and shows that, because it is only a part of the human being, the separated soul cannot be a person. To anyone whose knowledge of Thomism is sufficiently deep it is clear that the principle—the *ratio* of part is repugnant to that of personality—is an entirely general principle and is applied analogically depending on the case. Thus, John of St. Thomas shows, in speaking of the hypostatic union, which takes place in *persona* (*Sum. Theol.*, III, 2, 2.), that God can be united to human nature only as person just as He can be united to human intelligence only as *species intelligibilis* because in both cases He is united to them as term and as whole, not as part. (*Cursus Theol.*, De Incarnatione, Disput. IV, a. 1). The same principle must evidently come into play also—though under completely different conditions and following another line of application—when the notion of person is considered with respect to wholes which are no longer, like the human composite, substantial but have only an accidental unity, and are themselves composed of persons like the social whole.

of persons is to say that society is a whole composed of wholes. Taken in its full sense, this expression leads us directly to the society of the Divine Persons (for the idea of society is also an analogical idea). In the Divine Trinity, there is a whole, the divine Essence, which is the common good of the three subsisting Relations. With respect to this whole, the Three who compose the trinitarian society are by no means parts, since they are perfectly identical to it. They are three wholes who are the Whole. "Among created things," St. Thomas writes, "*one* is part of *two*, and *two* of *three* (as one man is part of two men, and two men of three). But it is not thus in God. For the Father is as much as the whole Trinity.[30]

We must be aware here of the irremediable deficiency of our language. Since our idea of society originates in and, as far as modes of conceptualization are concerned, is bound to our experience, the only possible way for us to express the fact that persons live in society is to say that they are parts of, or compose, society. But can it be said, except quite improperly, that the Divine Persons "are parts of" or "compose" the uncreated society? Here, precisely, where we are confronted

[30] *Sum. Theol.*, I, 30, ad 4.

with the society par excellence, a society of pure persons, our language is irremediably deficient. Let us keep in mind this essential point, which is the proper difficulty of and the key to the precisions to follow, namely that, if the person of itself requires "to be part of" society, or "to be a member of society," this in no wise means that it must be in society in the way in which a part is in a whole and treated in society as a part in a whole. On the contrary, the person, as person, requires to be treated as a whole in society.

To get the right idea of human society, we must consider it as located in the analogical scale between the uncreated exemplar, the super-analogue of the concept of society, namely, the divine society, except in an improper and metaphorical sense, namely, animal society. Infinitely above the city of men, there is a society of pure Persons, who are at the summit of individuality, but without the shadow of individuation by matter (or even by a form, distinct from the act of existence). Each one is in the other through an infinite communion,[31] the common good of which is strictly and absolutely the proper good of each, since it is that which each person is and their

[31] *Sum. Theol.*, I, 42, 5.

very act of existing. Far below the society of men, below even the level of all society properly so-called, there is a "society" of material individuals which are not persons, which are so isolated each within itself that they do not tend toward any communion and have no common good,[32] but each is totally subservient to the proper good of the whole. Human society is located between these two; a society of persons who are material individuals, hence isolated each within itself but nonetheless requiring communion with one another as far as possible here below in anticipation of that perfect communion with one another and God in life eternal. The terrestrial common good of such a society is, on the one hand, superior to the proper good of each member but flows back upon each. On the other hand, it sustains in each that movement by which it strives toward its own eternal good and the transcendent Whole; the same movement by which each goes beyond the order in which the common good of the terrestrial city is constituted.

. . . .

The person as such is a whole, an open and generous whole. In truth, if human society were

[32] In the formally social sense specified above pp. 39-40.

a society of *pure persons,* the good of society and
the good of each person would be one and the
same good. But man is very far from being a
pure person; the human person is the person of a
poor material individual, of an animal born more
helpless than any other animal. Though the person as such is an independent whole and that
which is noblest in all of nature, nonetheless the
human person is at the lowest degree of personality—naked and miserable, indigent and full
of wants. When it enters into society with its
kind, therefore, it happens that, by reason of its
deficiencies—evidences of its condition as an individual in the species—the human person is present *as part* of a whole which is greater and better
than its parts, and of which the common good
is worth more than the good of each part. Yet,
because of personality as such and the perfections
which it implies as an independent and open
whole, the human person requires membership
in society. Whence, as previously noted, it is essential to the good of the social whole to flow
back in some fashion upon the person of each
member. It is the human *person* who enters into
society; as an individual, it enters society as a

part whose proper good is inferior to the good of the whole (of the whole constituted of persons). But the good of the whole is what it is, and so superior to the private good, only if it benefits the individual persons, is redistributed to them and respects their dignity.

On the other hand, because it is ordained to the absolute and is summoned to a destiny beyond time, or, in other words, because of the highest requirements of personality as such, the human person, as a spiritual totality referred to the transcendent whole, *surpasses* and is superior to all temporal societies. From this point of view, or if you will, in respect to things *which are not Caesar's* both society itself and its common good are indirectly subordinated to the perfect accomplishment of the person and its supra-temporal aspirations as to an end of another order— an end which transcends them. A single human soul is worth more than the whole universe of material goods. There is nothing higher than the immortal soul, save God. With respect to the eternal destiny of the soul, society exists for each person and is subordinated to it.

We have just stated that the common good is

what it is only if it is redistributed to persons. Let us now add a consideration which is derived from the same principle but goes farther, namely, that the common good of the city or of civilization—an essentially human common good in which the whole of man is engaged—does not preserve its true nature unless it respects that which surpasses it, unless it is subordinated, not as a pure means, but as an infravalent end, to the order of eternal goods and the supra-temporal values from which human life is suspended.

This intrinsic subordination refers above all to the supernatural beatitude to which the human person is directly ordained. It is also and already related—a fact which a philosopher cannot ignore —to everything which of itself transcends political society, because all such things belong to the order of the absolute.[33] We have in mind the

[33] In this sense—because there do exist supra-temporal goods of the natural order (as, for example, the contemplative life as conceived by Aristotle)—it is perfectly true to say with Mortimer Adler and the Rev. Walter Farrell that the natural happiness of the human being transcends in certain essential elements the political common good (cf. Walter Farrell, O.P., "Person and the Common Good in a Democracy," *Proceedings of the American Catholic Philosophical Association,* Volume XX, December 27 and 28, 1945). These supra-temporal natural goods, by reason of which, even in the natural order, the human person transcends the State, are refracted imperfectly and diminishingly, in accordance with a certain social-temporal participation, in the political

natural law, the rule of justice and the requirements of fraternal love; the life of the spirit and all that which, in us, is a natural beginning of contemplation; the immaterial dignity of the truth, in all domains and all degrees however humble they may be, of theoretical knowledge, and the immaterial dignity of beauty, both of which are nobler than the things of common life and which, if curbed by it, never fail to avenge themselves. In the measure that human society attempts to free itself from this subordination and proclaim itself the supreme good, in the very same measure it perverts its own nature and that of the common good—in the same measure it destroys the common good. The common good of political society is an "honest good." But it is a practical good, and not the absolute good which, as we noted in the beginning, is the supreme

common good itself. (It is much the same with the supernatural virtues of the saints in so far as they add to the moral patrimony and glory of their temporal fatherland.) But of themselves, they are related to the order of civilization, and even more to the order of what, farther on, we call the community of minds. They are integrated in the common good of civilization (and this is "temporal" in contrast to the "spiritual" or supernatural order of the kingdom of God, but its highest natural values are "supra-temporal" or of the absolute order) and they arise directly out of the common good of the community of minds. Yet both the common good of civilization and that of the community of minds are themselves subordinated to the supernatural common good.

object of the theoretical intellect. The common good of civil life is an ultimate end, but an ultimate end in a relative sense and in a certain order. It is lost if it is closed within itself, for, of its very nature, it is intended to favor the higher ends of the human person. The human person's vocation to goods which transcend it is embodied in the essence of the common good. To ignore these truths is to sin at the same time and by the same token against both the human person and the common good.

When, against social pressures, the human person upholds right, justice, fraternal charity, when it raises itself above social life to enter into the solitary life of the spirit, when it deserts the banquets of common life, to feed upon the transcendentals, when, seeming to forget the city, it fastens to the adamantine objectivity of beauty and truth, when it pays obeisance to God rather than to men, in these very acts it still serves the common good of the city and in an eminent fashion.

And when the person sacrifices to the common good of the city that which is dearest to it, suffers torture and gives its life for the city, in these very acts because it wills what is good and acts in accordance with justice, it still loves its own soul, in accordance with the order of charity, more than the city and the common good of the city.

We see, then, that the true conception of political life is neither exclusively personalist nor exclusively communal. As we wrote many years ago, it is both personalist and communal in such a way that these two terms call for and imply one another. Hence, there is nothing more illusory than to pose the problem of the person and the common good in terms of opposition. In reality, it is posed in terms of reciprocal subordination and mutual implication.

Thus it is in the nature of things that man, as part of society, should be ordained to the common good and the common work for which the members of the city are assembled.[34] It is in the nature of things that he should, as the need arises, renounce activities which are nobler in themselves than those of the body politic for the salvation of the community. It is also in the nature of things that social life should impose numerous restraints and sacrifices upon his life as a person, considered as a part of the whole. But in the

[34] *The Rights of Man and Natural Law*, New York, 1943, pp. 39-43.

measure that these sacrifices and restraints are required and accepted in the name of justice and amity, they raise higher the spiritual level of the person. "Man finds himself by subordinating himself to the group, and the group attains its goal only by serving man and by realizing that man has secrets which escape the group and a vocation which the group does not encompass." [35]

And when, as we just noted, man freely accepts death, not as an enslaved fanatic or blind victim, but as a man and a citizen, for the sake of his people and his country, in that very act of extraordinary virtue, he affirms at the same time the supreme independence of the person in relation to the things of this world. In losing itself, in a temporal sense, for the sake of the city, the person sacrifices itself, in the most real and complete fashion. Yet the person is not defeated. The city still serves it because the soul of man is immortal and because the sacrifice gives grace one more chance.

We might observe in passing, that the sheer fact of existing is neither the supreme good nor any one of the absolute goods to which the person as such is ordained. It is, however, the first pre-

[35] *Ibid.*, p. 32.

requisite condition of the person's ordination to
these goods.[36] A human life is less precious than
the moral good and the duty of assuring the salvation of the community, is less precious than the
human and moral patrimony of which the community is the repository, and is less precious also
than the human and moral work which the community carries on from one century to the next.
It is, nonetheless, as the life of a person, superior
to every value of mere social utility. For it is the
life of a substance endowed with a spiritual soul
and possessing a right to its own existence. Not
the least paradox of our condition is the fact
that this good, which is metaphysically so precious, is by nature exposed, and even squandered,
in all manner of adventures—frequently for very
slight reasons. In the name of goods and interests,
which are only remotely connected with the
common good, society itself does not hesitate to
abuse it for any ends, even to waste it. The history of mankind is proof enough that human life,
as the life of an individual in the group, is in-

[36] For this reason, Christ could say of Judas: *"It were better
for him, if that man had not been born."* (Matt., 26, 24.) Of
course the act of existing never ceases to be *per se* good and
desirable; but *per accidens* it ceases to be so when it fails completely and lacks everything to which it is ordained. Cf. *Sum.
Theol.*, I, 5, 2, ad 3.

deed cheap. Only yesterday, across the Rhine, we saw to what atrocities a purely biological conception of society can lead. The destruction of human lives, which were believed to have become a burden on the community, was not only permitted, but even extolled.

In reality, the privilege connected with the dignity of the person is inalienable, and human life involves a sacred right. Whether to rid society of a useless member or for *raison d'état*, it is a crime to kill an innocent man. It is a crime to doom a prisoner to death in order to test some drugs which may save thousands of the sick. The social body does have the right, in a just war, to oblige its citizens to expose their lives in combat. It does not have the right to demand more than this risk, or to decree the death of a man for the salvation of the city. When it is a question of special missions in which men go to certain or almost certain death, volunteers are called for. This fact is itself an additional testimony to the right of the human person to life. Even in these extreme cases, something still bears witness to the transcendent value of human life in so far as it is the life of a person. The person can be obligated in conscience and, if necessary even constrained, to expose its life, but never can it be branded like an animal for the slaughterhouse. It is still as master of itself and by an act of virtue that it faces death. Apart from these ultimate demands of its dignity, it remains true that the person is duty-bound, in justice, to risk its own existence for the salvation of the whole when the whole is imperilled. It is so bound precisely because, as an individual, the person is in its entirety a part of the community from which, in a certain fashion, it has received all that it is. But it is thus obliged only because the terrestrial common good itself includes supra-human values and is indirectly related to the absolutely ultimate end of man. "If the common good of human society were uniquely and exclusively a sum of temporal advantages and achievements, like the common good—not really common but totalitarian—of an apiary or anthill, it would surely be nonsensical to sacrifice the life of a human person for it. Thus war, which pushes to the extreme limit the subordination of the individual person to the temporal community, at the same time attests the supra-temporal implications and supra-social finalities that this subordination presupposses. It can be seen, on the other hand, that, by reason of their very nature, the totalitarian states—the very states that devour human lives in the name of the nation—lose, as such, the right to ask of a man that he sacrifice his life for them." [37]

In short, though the person as such is a totality, the material individual, or the person as a material individual, is a part. Whereas the person, as person or totality, requires that the common good of the temporal society flow back over it, and even transcends the temporal society by its ordination to the transcendent whole, yet the person still remains, as an individual or part, inferior and subordinated to the whole and must, as an organ of the whole, serve the common work.

*   *   *

Two texts of St. Thomas, which supplement and balance one another, can guide us to a deeper penetration of these ideas. "Each individual person," St. Thomas writes, "is related to the entire community as the part to the whole." [38]

---

[37] *De Bergson à Thomas D'Aquin*, pp. 148-149.
[38] *Sum. Theol.*, II-II, 64, 2. Elsewhere too: "For, since one man is a part of the community, each man, in all that he is and has, belongs to the community; just as a part, in all that it is, belongs to the whole." I-II, 96, 4. "The person is compared to the community as a part to the whole." II-II, 61, 1. "The whole of man is directed as to his end to the whole of the community of which he is a part." II-II, 65, 1.

From this point of view and in this respect, that is because it is by reason of certain of its proper conditions a part of society, the person is in its entirety engaged in and ordained to the common good of society.

But let us add at once that, although man in his entirety is engaged as a part of political society (since he may have to give his life for it), he is not a part of political society *by reason of his entire self* and all that is in him. On the contrary, by reason of certain things in him, man in his entirety is elevated above political society. St. Thomas' second text that completes and balances the first is pertinent here; "Man is not ordained to the body politic according to all that he is and has." [39]

There is an enormous difference between this statement: "Man, by reason of certain things which are in him, is *in his entirety* engaged as a part of political society" and this other statement: "Man is part of political society *by reason of himself as a whole and by reason of all that is in him*." The first one is true, and the second one is false. Here lie both the difficulty and the solution

[39] "Man is not ordained to the body politic according to all that he is and has." *Sum. Theol.*, I-II, 21, 4, ad 3. "But all that man is, and can, and has, must be referred to God." *Ibid.*

71

of the problem. Anarchical individualism denies that man, by reason of certain things which are in him, is engaged in his entirety as a part of political society. Totalitarianism asserts that man is a part of political society by reason of himself as a whole and by reason of all that is in him ("all in the state, nothing against the state, nothing outside of the state"). The truth is that man is engaged in his entirety—but not by reason of his whole self—as a part of political society, a part ordained to the good of the society. In the same way, a good philosopher is engaged in his entirety in philosophy, but not by reason of all the functions and all the finalities of his being. He is engaged in his entirety in philosophy by reason of the special function and special finality of the intellect in him. A good runner engages the whole of himself in the race but not by reason of all the functions or all the finalities of his being. He engages the whole of himself in the race, but by reason of the neuromuscular machinery in him, not by reason of his knowledge of the Bible, for example, or of astronomy. The human person is engaged in its entirety as a part of political society, but not by reason of everything that is in it and everything that belongs to it. By reason of other things which are in the person, it is also in its entirety above political society. For in the person there are some things—and they are the most important and sacred ones—which transcend political society and draw man in his entirety above political society—the very same whole man who, by reason of another category of things, is a part of political society. By reason of certain relations to the common life which concern our whole being, we are a part of the state; but by reason of other relations (likewise of interest to our whole being) to things more important than the common life, there are goods and values in us which are neither by nor for the state, which are outside of the state.

Man is a part of and inferior to the political community by reason of the things in and of him which, due as they are to the deficiencies of material individuality, depend in their very essence upon political society and which in turn may be used as means to promote the temporal good of the society. In this sense, a mathematician has learned mathematics by reason of the educational institutions that social life alone makes possible. This progressive formation, which is received from others and is a proof of the limitations of the individual, depends upon the community. Consequently, the community can in given circumstances, require the mathematician to serve the social group by *teaching* mathematics.

On the other hand, by reason of the things in and of man, which are derived from the ordination of personality as such to the absolute and which thus depend in their essence on something higher than the political community and so concern properly the supra-temporal accomplishment of the person as person, man excells the political community. Thus mathematical truths do not depend upon the social community, but concern the order of the absolute goods of the person as such. The community will never have the right to require the mathematician *to hold as true* some one mathematical system rather than any other, or to teach such mathematics as is deemed to be more in conformity with the law of the social group (because they are, for instance, "Aryan" mathematics or "Marxist-Leninist" mathematics. . . .) [40]

Man is constituted a person, made for God and life eternal, before he is constituted a part of the

[40] Cf. *The Rights of Man and Natural Law*, p. 17.

city; and he is constituted a part of the family society before he is constituted a part of the political society. This is the origin of those primordial rights which political society must respect and which it may not injure when it requires the services of its members.

We have stated that, on the one hand, it is the person itself which enters into society and, on the other, that it is ultimately by reason of its material individuality that it is in society as a part whose good is inferior to the good of the whole. If that is the case, it is understandable that society cannot live without the perpetual gifts which come from persons, each one of whom is *irreplaceable* and incommunicable; and that, nevertheless, the very thing of persons which in social usage is retained is transmuted into something communicable and *replaceable,* always individualized but depersonalized.

We might add also that society, its life, and its peace, cannot subsist without that amity, namely, civil amity, which is the animating form of society [41] and essentially personal. However, the relations which make up the structure of society

[41] Cf. Gerald B. Phelan, "Justice and Friendship," in *The Maritain Volume of the Thomist* (New York, Sheed and Ward, Jan. 1943), pp. 153-170.

concern, as such, only *justice*, which is essentially impersonal because it is measured on things, and does not make acceptance of persons.

❖   ❖   ❖

From the above considerations we can draw two conclusions. The first concerns the mutual relations of the person and society. To characterize these relations we might make use of the following formulae: just as the person requires society both on account of its abundance or as a person, and on account of its poverty or as an individual, so the common good, by its very essence, directs itself to the persons as persons and directs the persons as individuals to itself. It directs itself to persons in a two-fold way: first, in so far as the persons are engaged in the social order, the common good by its essence must flow back over or redistribute itself to them; second, in so far as the persons transcend the social order and are directly ordained to the transcendent Whole, the common good by its essence must favor their progress toward the absolute goods which transcend political society. From the first point of view, we have the law of redistribution of the common good to the parts of society because these parts are persons. From the second point of view, we have the law of transcendence by which the transcendence of the person over society is manifested.

The second conclusion concerns the state of tension and conflict which is inherent in human society. Social life is naturally ordained—in the way in which we have tried to describe—to the good and the freedom of the person. And yet there is in this very same social life a natural tendency to enslave and diminish the person in the measure that society considers the person as a part and as a mere material individual. "When ever I have been among men," Seneca wrote, "I have come back less a man."

The person as person insists on serving the community and the common good freely. It insists on this while tending toward its own fullness, while transcending itself and the community in its movement toward the transcendent Whole. The person as an individual is necessarily bound, by constraint if need be, to serve the community and the common good since it is excelled by them as the part by the whole.

This paradox, this tension, and this conflict are something natural and inevitable. Their solution is not static but dynamic. For, in this way, a double movement is generated—a movement far more profound than the dialectical movement to which the Marxists appeal. The first of these movements is a dearly bought and ceaselessly hampered movement of the societies themselves as they develop in time. It is like a thrust—due above all to the energies of the spirit and of free-dom—across an ebb-tide in which the corruption, which belabors us, ceaselessly appears. For inso-far as it advances, this movement tends to realize gradually, in social life itself, man's aspiration to be treated as a person in the whole, or, if you will, as a whole and not as a part. To us this is a very abstract but exact expression of the ideal to which, from their inception, modern democracies have been aspiring, but which their philosophy of life has vitiated. This ideal, the complete realiza-tion of which cannot be expected here below, is an upper limit drawing to itself the ascending part of history. It calls for an heroic philosophy of life fastened to absolute and spiritual values. It can be gradually realized only by the develop-ment of law, of a kind of sacred sense of justice and honor, and by the development of civic amity. For justice and right, by imposing their law upon man as upon a moral agent and by appealing to reason and free will, concern, as such, personality; they transform into a relation between two wholes—the whole of the individual person and the social whole—that which otherwise would be no more than the pure subordination of the part to the whole. And love, by assuming voluntarily that which would otherwise be servitude, transfigures it into liberty and a free gift.[42]

The second movement is, so to speak, a vertical movement of the life of the persons themselves in the midst of social life. It arises out of the difference in altitude between the level where the person has the center of its life as a person and the level where it is constituted as a part of a social community. Because of this difference in level, the person demands society and always tends to go beyond it, "until, at last, it enters into a society of pure persons, that is, into the society of Divine Persons, which overwhelms it with the gift of

---

[42] Let us note here that just as the "extrinsic common good" of an army (victory) is superior to its "immanent common good," so the "extrinsic common good" of the social life of men in the course of terrestrial history (victory over servitude and the antagonisms that divide humanity) is superior to its "immanent common good" and completes its evolution. Out of this fact arises the historical dynamism which, through trials and disasters in the direction of an end, which perhaps will never be attained in the conditions of life here below, carries along with it the social forms of peoples and civilizations.

infinitely more than that to which it could of its own nature properly aspire. From the family group (which is more fundamental than the State because it touches upon the generic difference of the human being) man passes into civil society (which touches upon the specific difference) where he feels the need of clubs and fellowships that will interest his intellectual and moral life. These he enters of his own free choice; they assist the soul in its efforts to ascend to a higher level. In the end these also fail to satisfy —the soul is cramped and forced to go beyond them. Above the level of civil society, man crosses the threshold of supernatural reality and enters into a society that is the mystical body of an incarnate God—a society, the proper office of which is to lead him to his spiritual perfection and his full liberty of autonomy, to his eternal welfare. The Church is at once Desert and City.[43] Within her precincts, she nourishes human personality on a divine food and leads it away from the crowds at the circumference, where the soul finds contentment in life among men, towards the deeper solitude at the center, where it finds its highest contentment in life among the divine per-

[43] Cf. H. Clérissac, *Le Mystère de l'Eglise,* Chap. VI.

sons. At last, in the vision in which the intellect apprehends the Divine Essence, the person is more than ever lost in the life of the Church, but the common good of the Church is now unveiled and the human being, exalted by supernatural power to share as a pure personality in the Uncreated Society of the Divine Persons, enters into the Kingdom of God and the Light of Glory. Strive not, ye men, to socialize the life of the spirit. It tends of its own nature to live in society and finds its fulfillment only there." [44]

It will be noted that these considerations enable us to understand in its true sense the statement of Aristotle, so often repeated by St. Thomas and already alluded to at the beginning of this essay; the good of the city is more noble, *more divine* than that of the individual. Here, as on so many other points, Aristotle has expressed a remarkably pure principle whose significance could be penetrated only by eyes more illuminated than those of the pagan wisdom. This principle must be understood in a very precisely formal way; in the very same line of values in which the person is *a part* in relation to the social whole.

[44] Cf. Jacques Maritain, *Freedom in the Modern World*, 1936, pp. 51-52.

Then it is clear, as explained above, that the good of the community (the authentic and true common good) is superior to the good of the individual person *in the order of terrestrial values* according to which the person is a part of the community. But these values are not equal to the dignity and destiny of the person. By reason of the law of transcendence or transgression, which we have described, the person is raised to a higher level than the level at which it is but a part; at this level, the good of the person is the more elevated. However, at this higher level, it is still a part, but of a higher community, so that the *dictum authenticum* of Aristotle is verified anew, under altogether different conditions, and on an altogether different plane.

Thus in the natural order there is a community of minds in as much as minds communicate in the love of truth and beauty, in the life and work of knowledge, art and poetry, and in the highest values of culture. However, this community does not succeed in constituting itself as a society in the proper sense of the word, the kingdom of minds, as Leibnitz put it. We could speak of its common good only in an analogical sense. In fact, the common good of the intellects can be understood in two ways: in the first way, it is truth and beauty themselves, through the enjoyment of which minds receive a certain natural irradiation or participation of the Uncreated Truth and Beauty or of the separated common good. This common good of the intellects is obviously superior to the personal act by which each intellect conquers a fragment of it; but it is not a social good, a common good in the strict sense. This common good of the intellects is the immensity of the supra-temporal object, to some aspect of which, each adheres in solitude.

In the second way, the common good of the intellects is the intelligible treasure of culture in which minds communicate with one another. This treasure of culture, in relation to which minds accomplish a common work, more or less perfectly flows back over each of them. In this sense, it is undoubtedly a schema of social or common good in the strict sense—without an organized social body—and in a certain way, *extensive et diffusive,* it is something better than the proper good of each. From the point of view of extension, or from the point of view of the multiplicity by which the diverse aspects of the search for truth are manifested, it is better to have Plato, Aristotle, Kant and St. Thomas, than to have St. Thomas alone, even though, personally, we would be willing to dispense with all the others for St. Thomas. It is better to have Ruysbroeck and the pseudo-Dionysius, Gertrude and Catherine of Sienna, St. Theresa and St. John of the Cross than to have St. John of the Cross alone. But, absolutely speaking, the communion in which each mind enters, in a personal and solitary fashion, with truth through theoretical knowledge, and with God through contemplation, is better than the treasures of communicable culture which minds receive from one another. Thus the law of transcendence still holds with regard to the community of minds, as it does with regard to every human community. The person will still emerge above the community of minds and demand more, at least so long as the community in which it is engaged is not the supernatural society whose life is the communicated life of God—the Church herself, whose good is the same as the person's. There, in the community of the saints, the person no longer tends to emerge above the community and pass into a better society, for it is in the Church herself that its participation in the divine life is accomplished. Here, it is more than ever true that in different respects the person is for the community and the community is for the person. For there is for the Church a common work, which is continued redemption, to which each is ordained as the part to the work of the whole. But this common work is itself ordained to the personal good of each, to the union of each with God Himself, and to the application of the redeeming blood to each as a single person.

On the one hand, the proper good of the person as a person is achieved in the union of grace and charity with God, with the Uncreated Good, which is the Common Good of the Church—a transcendent common good which no longer is a practical good to be realized, but the subsisting good to which to adhere—above all human good and all communications of created goods found in the Church. In this sense, Francis de Vitoria wrote: "In the corporeal organism, the natural part exists directly for the whole. But in the Church, each man exists only for God and himself, at least directly and principally, because neither grace nor faith, nor hope, nor any other supernatural formality resides immediately in the entire community as in its subject." [45]

On the other hand, the proper good of the person, as an individual, that is, as a part of the created whole of which the head is the Incarnate Word, is inferior not only to the divine common Good of this whole, but also to the collection of human goods and of the communications of created goods which derive in this whole from its union of grace with the uncreated Good.

Thus, if we consider this grand City as living in its entirety upon a common good which is the very life of God, communicated to the multitude of the just and seeking out the errant, then each stone is for the city. But if we consider each stone as living itself, in its personal participation in this common good, upon the very life of God that is communicated, or as sought after personally by God, who wills to communicate His own life to it,

[45] "Besides, in the body, a natural part exists absolutely for the sake of the whole; in the Church, individual men exist for the sake of God and for themselves alone. Their private good is not ordained to the good of the whole at least formally or principally. As neither grace, nor faith, nor hope, nor any other supernatural forms reside immediately in the whole community, neither does the spiritual power, which is equally or even more supernatural." *De potestate Ecclesiae*, II, 5. Cf. Genito, *Relecciones del Maestro Fray Francisco de Vitoria*, Madrid, 1934, t. II, p. 117.

then it is toward each one that all the goods of
the city converge to flow back in the measure of
his capacity to receive of their plenitude. In this
sense, the city is for each stone. It is for each of
God's saints, St. Thomas writes, that it is spoken
in Matthew: "He shall place him over all His
goods." [46] And of each, St. John of the Cross
writes: "Mine are the heavens and mine the
earth, mine are all men, the just and the wicked;
the angels are mine and the Mother of God, all
things are mine; God Himself is mine and for me.
What then dost thou demand and after what dost
thou seek, oh my soul? For thine is all of this, and
all of this is for thee." [47]

Finally, in the beatific vision, through the intuition of the divine essence, each blessed soul
becomes God, in an intentional way, as Cajetan
says, and thus enters into the uncreated society
of the Divine Persons. The proper eternal good
of each, in the degree that its vision grasps it, is
the common Good itself of the Divine Persons.
Each beholds but does not "comprehend" it, for
it still exceeds infinitely the capacity of each. And
each one loves it more than itself. Further, be-

[46] Saint Thomas, *Expos. in Ep. ad Rom.*, c. 8, lect. 6.
[47] Saint John of the Cross, *Avisos y Sentencias* (ms. d'Andujar),
Silv. IV, p. 235.

87

cause there is a multitude of blessed souls which partake of the same uncreated Good, this Good actually becomes the common Good of both the Divine Persons and the Church of Heaven. Being God Himself, it is of course *more divine* than the act, entitatively considered, by which each created member of the heavenly community, according to the degree of its vision, takes possession of its personal good, (which, be it noted, is more really the good of the created person since it excels it infinitely). But in what sense might the personal good, of which each soul thus takes possession, be inferior to this common good? They are identical; the personal good is also God Himself. In relation to the divine service and the divine praise, each soul is a part of the community of the blessed. In relation to the object of the vision, there is no longer a question of being a part but of being identified with the Whole in this society of the blessed, the common object of which is better only because it is, for the multitude of the members, the same object in which each one shares, though in different degrees, as a whole identified with the Whole. Here, in the intentional identification of each soul with the divine essence, the law of the primacy of the common good over the personal good comes to an end in a certain sense.[48] And it comes to an end here precisely because the personal good *is* at that moment the common good. "The personal good of each of the blessed is *as divine* as the separated common Good of the entire universe: it is *identically* this very same Good, spiritually possessed."[49]

[48] In another sense, this law always holds; in the sense that the infinite communicability of the incomprehensible Essence forever transcends the communication which, through its vision, the creature receives of it.

[49] Charles Journet, "La cause matérielle de l'Eglise glorieuse," *Nova et Vetera*, January-March, 1945, p. 86.

V

---◆---

Contemporary Problems

LET us consider briefly what becomes of the person in those political philosophies which are based upon a materialistic conception of the world and life. Three things must be distinguished in the consideration of any philosophy: first, the sentimental values which lure the reason or the simply human aspirations to which its adherents actually, even though unwittingly, respond; secondly, what the philosophy itself *states*; thirdly, what it *does* and the results to which it leads.

We hold that every materialistic philosophy of man and society is drawn, in spite of itself (in virtue of the real aspirations of its followers who, after all, are men), by the values and goods proper to personality. Even when ignoring them, such doctrines obscurely desire these values and goods so that in practice they can act upon men only by invoking justice, liberty, the goods of the person.

But what do they express, considered as doctrines? Blind to the realities of the spirit, responsive only to what belongs to the world of matter, they see in man no more than the shadow of true personality, his material individuality. This alone in man are they able to express. Actually, they jeopardize the person either by dissolving it in anarchy or, as inexorably happens under the pressure of political necessities, by subjecting it to the social body as Number, economic community, national or racial state.

Here, we can only indicate the appropriate criticism of the materialistic philosophy of society in its three principal forms; bourgeois individualism, communistic anti-individualism, totalitarian or dictatorial anti-communism and anti-individualism. All three disregard the human *person* in one way or another, and, in its place, consider, willingly or not, the *material individual* alone.

❋   ❋   ❋

It has been frequently noted that bourgeois liberalism with its ambition to ground everything

91

in the unchecked initiative of the individual, conceived as a little God, and the absolute liberty of property, business and pleasure, inevitably ends in statism. The rule of the Number produces the omnipotence of the state. The indispensable condition for building a city out of liberties, beholden only to themselves, is that each member surrender his personal will to the General Will in a contract, which, according to Rousseau, gives birth to society. But since man in his material individuality is a part, not a whole, and since, further, in this system, the state takes the place of the genuine community, the individual is forced ultimately to transfer both his responsibilities and the care of his destiny to the artificial whole which has been superimposed upon him and to which he is bound mechanically. Of course his liberty will remain complete and unhampered, but in an illusory fashion and in a world of dreams. At the same time, he will exact from the state the satisfaction of his greeds and anarchistically reject the conditions of social life; not realizing that in this way society is driven to the insurrection of the parts against the whole, of which Auguste Comte used to speak, to the tragic isolation of each one in his own selfishness or helplessness. The very notion of the common good and the common work disappears.

Communism can be considered a reaction against such individualism. It claims to be directed towards the absolute emancipation of man, destined, in this system, to become the God of history. At its very origin, we find a desperate protest against the dehumanization of the person. But the person which it strives to liberate is conceived as purely immanent in the group. Hence the only emancipation which it could, in reality, achieve, would be that of the collective man, not at all that of the individual person. Further, if the political state is to be abolished in the end, as Marx held, society, as the economic community in the broadest sense, would subordinate the whole life of the persons to itself. A radical prejudice against all transcendence has, from its inception, forced communism to disregard the person as person and, as a consequence, the proper function of civil society as a city of human persons. This function is to procure an essentially human common good which includes, as its principal value, the free expansion of the individual persons together with all the guarantees required by this freedom. Under the pretext of substituting for the government of men the administration of things, Communism has made of this administration, which embraces the productivity of the mind as well as that of manual labor, the *principal* work of civil society. By an inescapable law, civil society marshals for its own work the human life of the persons. Where the primary aim of the marshaling is no longer to procure the freedom of expansion of the persons but simply the good and maximum production of the economic whole, this life inevitably finds itself referred in its entirety to that production and the society which procures it.

Anti-communistic and anti-individualistic reactions of the totalitarian or dictatorial type seek to incorporate man in all his being into a social whole composed of a multitude of material individualities rather than true persons. They seek this in the name of the state's sovereign dignity, the spirit of the people or the race and blood rather than in the name of the social community and the liberty of the collective man. Here the multitude becomes conscious of itself and symbolizes its omnipotence unto itself in the person of a Master, the only person, after all, in the political life above the "organized" aggregate of material individualities. It cannot be said that, in such a system, the emancipation of the person is sought along a wrong track; it is squarely rejected and abominated. The person as person is the enemy.

We note, in all three cases, a conflict between the whole and the part: at one time social life is destroyed by the individual whose selfishness looks to the state machinery for everything; now it swallows up the individual's hopes; now it annihilates his liberty and dignity by crushing him. Thus in different ways, all that is proper to the human person as person and to society as the city of persons is eliminated.

Our own day, we might add, seems to witness the tragedy of these three conflicting forms of social and political materialism. The moral crisis of our occidental civilization and the disastrous spasms of our liberal, capitalistic economy exhibit all too clearly the tragedy of bourgeois individualism.

The tragedy of Communism is most strikingly exposed in the dialectical back-slidings, the perpetual political regimentation, to which its own realizations in Russia have forced it, and in the internecine conflicts which it cannot but generate. From this point of view, the successive waves of terror which sweep over the Soviet Republics are of special significance to the philosopher. As a kind of economic theocracy, Communism requires a very powerful and rigorous discipline, which it can generate only through the external processes of thought control and constraint. Yet without a certain interior ethic recognizing and respecting the aspirations of the soul and the person, without an intelligent faith able to communicate its impulse from mind to mind, no strong social discipline can be freely accepted. Thus an internal conflict arises inevitably between the ever-resurgent anarchy of passions, ambitions, individual energies, grasping every means, and an "order" which ignores the principle of order. Sometimes an appeal is made to this interior ethic and intelligent faith, whose necessity has been understood, but, once aroused, they in turn become a threat to the self-enclosed whole which has taken advantage of them after having awakened them.

The tragedy of the national totalitarian states consists principally in this; while they require the total devotion of the person, they lack and even repudiate explicitly all understanding and respect for the person and its interior riches. In consequence, they are impelled to seek a principle of human exaltation in myths of outward grandeur and unending efforts toward external power and prestige. Such an impulse tends of itself to generate war and the self-destruction of the civilized community. (This observation was easy enough on the eve of the second World War, when these lines were written, but, today, it is awesomely verified after the collapse of these states—at long last extinguished but at so great a price!)

A final remark, relative to the attitude of these political philosophies toward Christianity, is appropriate at this point. Of the three, the most irreligious is bourgeois liberalism. Christian in appearance, it has been atheistic in fact. Too sceptical to persecute, except for a tangible profit, rather than defy religion, which it deemed an invention of the priesthood and gradually dispossessed by reason, it used it as a police force to watch over property, or as a bank where anyone could be insured, while making money here below, against the undiscovered risks of the hereafter—after all, one never knows!

The other two defied Christianity, but the metaphysical positions in this defiance disclosed

altogether different roots and meanings. The national totalitarian states, whose ideology lives
after them, heirs of the ancient antagonism of the
pagan Empire against the Gospel, represented an
external force arrayed against Christianity to enslave or to annihilate it in the name of the di-
vinized political Power. In the temporal order,
they opposed an irrational philosophy of enslave-
ment to both the genuine principle and the parasitical illusions of democracy. Communism, on
the contrary, in spite of the materialistic philosophy in which it finds its conceptual expression,
and which blinds it to its own essential content,
belongs to the historical trend of modern ration-
alism; a trend of anthropocentric humanism, of
democratic aspirations regulated by immanentist
dogmas and engaged in an ideological struggle
with their own Christian origins. Of this whole
historical trend, Communism is the final episode.
In reality, then, it must be counted a Christian
heresy—the ultimate and altogether radical Christian heresy. Like the Church, it is universalist.
In its militants, it stirs energies which, though
now entirely secularized, remain Christian in origin. The transformation of man which Christianity seeks in an interior grace renewing the person

for both time and eternity, Communism seeks
in the collective revolution renewing history and
society only for the life here-below. Its atheism
is an ethical and religious rancor against the
divine transcendence. It fights its own battle on
the very ground upon which Christianity has its
foundations. And it carries on this battle, which
consists in a process of substitution and super-
cession rather than aggression, from within Christian civilization as though, in its own secret
estimate of itself, the only true Christians (here-
below and delivered from the transcendent God)
were the Communists. As a result, Communists
and Christians, in their mutual relations, have a
bad conscience. Even when they sincerely offer
the "out-stretched hand" to the Catholics, the
Communists feel obscurely that their vocation is
to supplant them in political life and civilization.
Catholics, however, know very well that they risk
being replaced and that the "outstretched hand"
lures them into a land which is not that of their
faith. They recognize it clearly as a land of terrestrial activity in which too often, in the past,
they have neglected their temporal mission, and
which now, in the name of revolution, is erected
into a supreme end. And, while Communism

advances, accusing indiscriminately their faith and their omissions, while militant atheism reflects, as in a mirror of flame, the cruel image of that practical atheism of which so many of their own have been guilty, they sense, with a kind of anxiety, that normally it would be for them, who possess the words of eternal life, to stretch out the hand to the Communists and draw them into that land, which is first and above all their own, the land of religious truth and redemptory love.

May the time still be theirs to do it! On the level of terrestrial things, where in our times the working class has just about reached its historical maturity, may they prove able to keep alive the Christian ideal and Christian effort, pure and whole, in the common work of men and in the transforming movement that is taking place in society! May this be theirs that one day they might give to this movement of transformation the inspiration that will animate it, or at least, even in tribulation, conserve for it the essentials of its spiritual heritage!

Materialistic conceptions of the world and life, philosophies which do not recognize the spiritual and eternal element in man cannot escape error in their efforts to construct a truly human society

100

because they cannot satisfy the requirements of the person, and, by that very fact, they cannot grasp the nature of society. Whoever recognizes this spiritual and eternal element in man, recognizes also the aspiration, immanent in the person, to transcend, by reason of that which is most sublime in it, the life and conditions of temporal societies. Thus temporal society can be erected in accordance with the proper laws of its own nature. Its genuine character as a society of persons is understood. The natural tendency of the person to society, and the relation by which it morally and legally belongs to the society of which it is a part are also understood.

In the final analysis, the relation of the individual to society must not be conceived after the atomistic and mechanistic pattern of bourgeois individualism which destroys the organic social totality, or after the biological and animal pattern of the statist or racist totalitarian conception which swallows up the person, here reduced to a mere histological element of Behemoth or Leviathan, in the body of the state, or after the biological and industrial pattern of the Communistic conception which ordains the entire person, like a worker in the great human hive, to the proper

101

work of the social whole. The relation of the individual to society must be conceived after an irreducibly human and specifically ethicosocial pattern, that is, personalist and communalist at the same time; the organization to be accomplished is one of liberties. But an organization of liberties is unthinkable apart from the *moral* realities of *justice* and *civil amity,* which, on the natural and temporal plane, correspond to what the Gospel calls brotherly love on the spiritual and supernatural plane.

This brings us back to our considerations of the manner in which the paradox of social life is resolved in a progressive movement that will never be terminated here-below. There is a common work to be accomplished by the social whole as such. This whole, of which human persons are the parts, is not "neutral" but is itself committed and bound by a temporal vocation. Thus *the persons are subordinated to this common work.* Nevertheless, not only in the political order, is it essential to the common good to flow back upon the persons, but also in another order where that which is most profound in the person, its supra-temporal vocation and the goods connected with it, is a transcendent end, it is essential that *society itself and its common work are indirectly subordinated.* This follows from the fact that the principal value of the common work of society is the freedom of expansion of the person together with all the guarantees which this freedom implies and the diffusion of good that flows from it. In short, the political common good is a common good of human persons. And thus it turns out that, in subordinating oneself to this common work, by the grace of justice and amity, each one of us is still subordinated to the good of persons, to the accomplishment of the personal life of *others* and, at the same time, to the interior dignity of ones own person. But for this solution to be practical, there must be full recognition in the city of the true nature of the common work and, at the same time, recognition also of the importance and political worth—so nicely perceived by Aristotle—of the virtue of amity.

Such an historical ideal responds to the most profound aspirations of human nature and the rational requirements of a sound political philosophy. It is difficult not to think that its realization—powerfully opposed by the lower forces of our nature and the difficulties which reason encounters in its endeavor to establish its rule among us—would be the consequence and terrestrial projection, as it were, of that awareness of the dignity of the human person and the eternal vocation in every man, which the Gospel has imprinted in the heart of humanity.

On the other hand, there are grounds for believing that in the historical development of civilization there is in fact produced a slow, spontaneous activation of the mass of humanity and its secular conscience which tends to orientate men's desires towards just such an ideal through the failures, which seem to give it the lie, and the counterfeits which, like the individualistic liberalism of the XIXth Century, threaten to arouse mighty reactions against it. At any rate, how can we fail to see that it cannot be realized apart from that elevation which nature and civilizations receive, in their own order, from the energies of the Christian life? In this light, the tendency towards the materialism and atheism inherent in *the city of the individual* appears as cne of the absurdities by which it destroys itself. In the political order, the internal dialectic of this tendency, by a similar absurdity, drags it towards dictatorship which is its proper negation.

These reflections lead us to believe that the drama of the modern democracies has consisted in the unwitting quest of something good, the city of the persons, masked by the error of the city of the individual, which, by nature, leads to dreadful liquidations. It is not for the philosophers to forecast whether they can yet reorientate themselves decisively in the direction of the truth which they seek by disengaging the parasitical errors from their quest. Such a reorientation would presuppose a radical transformation and a vast return towards the spirit.

INDEX OF PROPER NAMES